Full Moon Clinic

by

JULIE WIRE

PAGE PUBLISHING, INC.
New York, NY

First originally published by Page Publishing, Inc. 2015

ISBN 978-1-68139-137-3 (pbk)
ISBN 978-1-68139-138-0 (digital)

Printed in the United States of America

Contents

The Beginning

My first job in veterinary medicine was an animal care attendant. Many memories come to mind. Shortly after I started, I remember bathing a huge German Shepherd. Great dog. Everything went fine, although the next day when I woke up, I could not open my eyes, and I was covered in a rash. I came to find out I had gotten poison ivy from the dog! Lots of steroids and cream and in a week, I was good to go again!

As a technician, a vivid memory was the beginning of the parvo era. Parvo was a highly contagious virus that caused explosive vomiting and diarrhea. And there was no specific treatment, nor was there a vaccine at this time. We just supported the dog with alot of fluids and injectable antibiotics and hoped for the best. You always knew when you opened the door to the hospital ward what kind of day you would have. First, parvo had a very distinguished smell, and what came next was really gross! Dogs would have diarrhea so explosive that would literally shoot from one side of the room to the other.

The first parvo case we had was with a Puli. These are dogs that look like a body covered in dreadlocks, and he looked like a string mop. His name was Jaqi Pu, and he was a show dog. Due to his show status, his owner would not permit us to shave his legs for an IV catheter. You can only imagine the trouble we had in keeping this dog treated, and due to the vomiting and diarrhea, we would be constantly bathing him, but he *never* dried! Jaqi Pu did survive, but many dogs did not.

Along with not knowing how to treat this virus, no one knew how to clean and disinfect the cages, runs, etc. So what did we use? Bleach, of course. And no one also knew the proper dilution, so you guessed. I remember our eyes and noses burning and difficulty breathing.

Amazing we all survived the parvo era!

Mindy, "the Torpedo"

This is a story I will never forget as well. Keep in mind there were no cell phones yet.

It was a very cold, snowy, icy day in January. I was working as a manager and teched when I was needed. It was a time where I knew every client in the practice and loved it! Early on a Monday, Mr. Trimmer walked in, sobbing. He told us he had a serious house fire overnight and his dog, Mindy, died in the fire, but she was still in the house. He said he needed to get her out and *now*! He asked if I would come and help him. Dumb me said sure; I knew where he lived, and it was not far.

I got my coat and took some blankets and gloves, and we left in his El Camino. As he started driving, I smelled alcohol. I asked him if he had been drinking and said, "Yeah, a little." Just great! Luckily, his house was only about three miles away, and we arrived safely. He lived alone in one of those big old half-houses, and it looked pretty badly burned.

As we entered, the bottom floor wasn't too bad, but as we started up the stairs, things got much worse. Everything was burnt, there was water dripping everywhere, and there was yellow tape hanging. Again, I asked, "Are we allowed to be here?" He responded, "It's my house, and I'll do as I want." I was not feeling too good now. He said she was in the front bedroom, and we slowly made our way. Floors were sagging and creaking. We entered the bedroom, and the bed was upside down. He said, "She's under the bed." OMG! Of course, all the windows were broken, and there was glass everywhere. We slowly made our way over, and using the blanket and gloves, we turned the bed over, and sure enough, there she was! Now Mindy was a Lab and weighed at sixty-five to seventy pounds. Now she was bloated and covered in glass as well. I was thinking to myself, *What have I gotten myself into?* Mr. Trimmer was sobbing and was of not much use. Don't ask me how, but I got her on the blanket and covered her. I then told him we have to get out of here and quick and asked him to grab an end of the blanket, and we started back toward the stairs. He stopped and broke down again. The floor was sagging, and I said, "We *have* to hurry."

He gained composure, and as we started going down the stairs, I told him I'll take lead and all he had to do was support the back end. We got halfway down the stairs, and he started sobbing again and let go, and she shot out of the blanket and down the stairs and hit the door, crashes through the door, out onto the frozen porch, and landed on the front sidewalk!

Again, OMG! We raced out the door, and he was absolutely a mess. I covered her up again and cut my hand on millions of shreds of glass lying all over her. There was a minimart right across the street, and a customer came out the door just as Mindy torpedoed out the door. He was just standing there with his mouth open and big eyes. I yelled for him to come help me, and he slowly crossed the street and asked, "What the heck just happened?" I quickly explained and got Mindy back in the car. I told Mr. Trimmer that I'm *driving*. He's sobbing as we drove back to the hospital. I parked the car at the back where the garage that housed the freezer was and went inside the hospital.

I'm covered in black soot, freezing in wet clothing and my hand bleeding. And what happened? Due to my wet shoes, I fell flat on my butt! As the staff came running, all I could do was lie there and laugh, and laugh, and laugh. I finished taking care of Mindy and drove Mr. Trimmer to a friend's house. True story!

Ebony versus Ivory

We had a client who had euthanized their old cat "Whitey." They were very upset and decided to come back the next day to pick up the cat to bury it at their farm. I was not at the hospital when they had the procedure done. As most hospitals, we had a body freezer, and all staff were taught to mark the bodies very carefully. Well, the next day, the owner came back to retrieve the body, and I was the one who took care of him. The chart said "Body is on the ledge in the freezer in the white box." Okay, fine, I went back, and sure enough, there it was. I took it to the car for the client and shared my sympathy with him.

An hour later, he showed back up and asked to talk to me. He had the box in his hands. As I took him into an exam room, I, of course, did not have a good feeling about this. He turned and started laughing and said, "Well, I came to pick up Whitey, but doc never told me they turn colors when they die. This cat is all black. Now I don't think this cat is Whitey, but she sure is pretty, and I wish old Whitey had looked like this." I thought I was going to die of embarrassment. Needless to say, I called an emergency staff meeting to discuss the importance of marking pets correctly. This could have ended up much worse, if not for the understanding and humor of the owner.

Into the Depths

I truly believe that all veterinarians have some "hoarding" in their blood, from keeping a "cute sign," toys from a deal, broken computers, and blood machines, saying, "Well, we can probably use the parts sometime." I have cleaned a lot of sheds, basements, and closets in my time, but there is one that stands out among the rest.

There was a practice, in which, the founding owner, who was great to work for, had a *big* case of being a hoarder. His desk was proof. We could never find anything in the mess, but he seemed to know where every piece of information was. He retired and did clean his desk, and there were mounds of boxes and bags that went out of the office. This was all fine, but the basement of this practice was severely out of control. I kept asking him to go through things and tell me what he wanted to keep, but he just kept putting me off and off. Finally, after two years, the fire marshal made a visit and put his foot down, stating the basement was a fire hazard and *had* to be cleaned. *Yeah!*

Well, it was decided to get in a two-ton trash bin, and we set off to work. The owner did go down and tell me some of the things he wanted but trusted me to put aside anything I thought he might like. As we began, considering you could barely walk, it was quite a daunting task. Many staff helped me, and we started at the base of the steps and slowly worked our way through. Bag after bag of junk went back up the stairs. When the foot of the stairs was clean, we all shouted! But then the *real* work began. We started going through all the stuff toward the back of the basement, boxes of antiquated equipment (some of which I did put back for the owner to go through), old dried-up paint cans, hundreds of old veterinary instruments, and yes, even a sink and the plumbing to go with it. More bottles of various sizes and shapes than I had ever seen, and some turned out to be precious finds for many of us. One of the more "unique" finds were small lab bottles that actually looked like meth pipes. We all got a chuckle out of them. So many hardworking staff helped, and more trips up the stairs we went, filling the bin. Leaving work one day when the first bin was almost full proved to be a hoot. While I was walking to my car, there were two of my dear staff *in* the bin, going through things. It seemed one wanted the plumbing items for her garden, and the other wanted some cabinets. As the saying goes, "One man's junk is another's treasure."

We filled the first bin in no time, and much more work was to be done. It was at this time, along with some prized possessions, we also found the worst of the worst. Many dead mice, old wood and paneling covered in crud and mold and grime you cannot imagine. During this time, I ruined two sets of clothing, carrying these things up the stairs and one day becoming quite ill suddenly. I shuddered to think what I breathed in, but luckily, I recovered overnight. The second bin arrived, and we continued on. You have to realize all our normal work was still there; we just had to try and find times to "continue to work on the basement." We were vigilant and started to really see results. Now it was getting exciting. The last area we cleaned was under the steps. We all thought, "No big deal." Ha! An unbelievable amount of stuff, and part of it was an antiquated scale in a big case. Really cool. We also found a huge old army trunk, and in it were hundreds of old veterinary books and journals. Quite impressive, but heavy as hell, carrying them up the stairs. The last large item we found was a lovely old door, which was in surprisingly good shape. So many of us wanted that old door, but just couldn't make it work anywhere. So it was put on top of the second trash bin, and off it went. We had filled four tons of space from this basement!

It was such a remarkable feeling to see the transformation of this old cluttered basement to this clean well-organized area. Gosh, we were all so proud of what we had done. During the seven weeks this project took, none of the owners had anything to say. Never a "thank you," "good job," nothing. Well, my wonderful staff filled out a "Catch me at my best" form, thanking me for my part in the cleaning project and gave it to Dr. Green. During our weekly doctors' meeting, she got it out and said she had been given it to give to me. I was so touched that my friends would think of me. And her comment was, "I think it's just funny." And that was it. Neither of the other two owners had anything to say. I have kept this lovely piece of paper and its meaning.

Gosh, after writing this, I guess I could also put this story in my chapter, "Not such a great boss," huh?

Joe

One of the best tricks I ever pulled off involved my maintenance man, Joe. Joe was a wonderful hardworking guy who was African American. He had always stated how he was deadly afraid of snakes. One summer day, I happened to find a dead snake outside our large-animal barn. It was just a garter snake, about twelve inches long. My mind went to work. One of Joe's many duties was to deliver supplies to our other three locations, and he used our company truck. So my plan was to wait until he had the truck all loaded, then have someone distract him inside while I went out and planted the snake. I draped it over the steering wheel, and it looked so real! Then I went back in and waited.

There were a bunch of us by this time, and we could see the truck very well as we hid by the back door. Joe opened the door and got in. We saw his hands fly up; he screamed, opened the door, and actually fell out of the truck! Well, we could not stop laughing, and we ran out to the truck. He looked up, saw us busting our guts, realized "he's been had," and started to laugh and said, "You guys . . . I think I just turned white!" We all laughed for a very, very long time over this one.

Love ya, Joe!

Dr. Perkin's Birthday Ride

It was Dr. Perkins birthday, and we decided to take him to lunch, but not in the usual way. Oh, we told him not to plan anything for two hours over lunch, but that's all we said. We started out by blindfolding him, and he was to guess where we were going to take him. We loaded him into Dr. Wheat's van and drove all over Hoovertown on every back road we could find. Once we got back on Main Street, we also opened all the windows and held a toy gun to his head. Of course, he had no idea, but the looks we got from everyone we passed were priceless. We just could not stop laughing. We ended up at Lions Pride in Hoovertown. Dr. Perkins said he had no idea where we were.

Walking him into the restaurant, still blindfolded and still at gunpoint with the kid's gun, the entire crowd started hollering and laughing. Dr. Perkins was very well-known in the community, and everyone also knew he had a great sense of humor. We then asked him if he wanted to wash his hands before lunch, and he said yes. So we put his hands under the soda fountain, and he washed his hands with Coke! The folks in the restaurant were going nuts! We then removed the blindfold, and when Dr. Perkins saw where he was, he also started to laugh hysterically as the crowd gave him a standing ovation. This was a birthday he would never forget!

Oh, the Things I Have Done for Veterinarians

Helped hire a nanny
Took their kids to school
Baked pies for their dinner party
Took their clothes to the cleaner
Pushed and shoveled their cars out of snow
Purchased flowers for their garden
Destroyed bee and wasp nests
Cleaned out their basement
Babysat
Took their kids to the doctors and dentist and airport
Took the doctor's wife to the doctor and admitted her to the
hospital
Cleaned out gutters
Mowed grass
Repaired power washers
Did laundry and iron
Scrubbed floors
Changed air filters
Purchased liquor for them

You name it, I've probably done it.

T-Bird

It was a cool fall evening, and I had just worked a very long day. At the time, I was driving a 1972 Thunderbird. This car was humongous in all ways. At this particular hospital, I backed the car in, so pulling out was not as challenging, and the parking lot was right in front of the hospital. At this time, no one ever locked their cars.

I was the last to leave and got in my car and turned it on. All of a sudden, I heard a startling loud scream. It scared the heck out of me, and I hit the accelerator and almost ran right into the practice. Then, I hit the brakes and just sat there for a moment to collect myself.

All of a sudden, a small fuzzy kitten was crawling up my neck from the backseat. I grabbed it, and it was a very young orange tiger. I was pretty upset and took the kitten back into the hospital.

It was absolutely filthy, covered in fleas and tar, ears filled with mites and a swollen belly. I put it in a cage with food, water, and litter and left. I could not believe someone would dump a kitten in my car.

I went in the next day, cleaned him up, wormed him, and was bound to find him a home.

Of course, three days later, I took him home and named him "T-Bird." It ended up being one of my most favorite cats, and he lived to be a ripe sixteen years old!

I never did find out who put him in my car, but now I am grateful!

A Match Made Where?

While working as a manager in a practice that included large-animal medicine, we hired a new associate named Tom. He was very nice, had strong faith, and there was just something about him I liked. He and I would talk at the end of some of his days, he describing his "challenging" cases, and I would do the same, only most of mine involved clients. At this same time, my daughter, Claire, was working with youth at a church in Maryland. Claire had called me one night and said, "Just talk to me, I need some adult conversation."

The next day, Tom came in, sat down, and said, "Do you know anywhere I could meet some new friends?" And I replied that my daughter was close to his age and needed some adult conversation. I said that perhaps I could ask her if they could exchange e-mails. He said he would be interested. I told Claire about him, and she agreed to the exchange. They spoke and e-mailed a few weeks and did meet briefly when Claire had come to town to do some shopping.

It was now December, and I had gotten tickets for both my daughters and my mother to go to Sight & Sound Theatre. Two days before the show, my youngest daughter, Keely, called and said she was too ill from morning sickness to attend. I called Claire and asked her if she wanted to find someone else to go. The day of the show, Tom walked in and announced that *he* was coming to the show with us! I could not believe it! Here I was with my mother, and we were all going together. I was thinking, *Awkward*.

My mother and I arrived at the theatre and looked for Claire. We finally saw her, and she looked different. She had gotten her hair highlighted, and I wasn't sure Tom would recognize her. But sure enough, he arrived and we all went in. The show was fantastic, and by intermission, Tom and Claire seemed to be having a great time chatting away.

The show ended, I took my mother home, and on the way she said how much she liked him too. She turned to me and said, "Well, you know, there is always a lid for every pot." I just cracked up laughing.

I'm happy to report the relationship blossomed, and they eventually got married!

Chico

Early on in my career as a technician, we were used to working on dogs and cats only. But occasionally, we would see a bird. One I so remember was Chico. He was a twenty-year-old African grey, who had quite a vocabulary. He had come in to board and had stayed for two weeks. During that time, he learned to bark like a dog and meow like a cat. Hilarious was all I can say to describe him. We would trim his beak and nails, and he would say "Thank you soooo much."

His owner became quite ill and asked if we would keep Chico for an extended period of time, and we were delighted. We kept him in the reception, and he provided such entertainment for the clients. His vocabulary grew and grew, and he could mimic anyone, and we just marveled. All the pets would sit and watch him and seem to be mesmerized. Even the dogs.

I learned so much about birds that summer, and some of us would take Chico home for weekends. My family thoroughly enjoyed him, and he would just walk around the house, talking constantly. My dog and cats were not afraid and would follow him around too. We all just laughed and laughed, and then he would laugh too!

Eventually, his owner did recover and took him home, but our hospital was not the same. We all couldn't wait to see Chico again and begged his owner to board him again. He did so frequently, and it was a wonderful experience I will not forget!

Hard to Believe

As hard as it is to believe, there were owners who drop their pets off for various reasons and never return.

One such save was Yin. She was a four-year-old female Siamese cat. Her owners brought her in to be euthanized because she "meowed too much"! I always loved Siamese cats, and cats that talked. There was no way I was going to let her be put down, so I asked the owners if I could provide a good home for her. Luckily, they agreed. Yin was a delight, and we all thoroughly enjoyed her talking.

It was a beautiful fall day in October, and we had recently moved into our new home. We were planting trees and shrubs and had the garage doors wide open. There was another room on the other side of the garage that we would eventually make into a rec room, but there was no door there yet.

As we came in for lunch, we came through the garage to remove our shoes. We saw this weird thing in the door leading to the upstairs, and there was blood everywhere! Further examination revealed it was about four inches of a cat's tail. We climbed the stairs, seeing blood all over our new walls. We followed the trail and entered my daughter's bedroom. And there was Yin, lying on the bed, talking, swishing what was left of her tail and blood everywhere. We figured the wind had blown the door shut, and she was in the wrong place at the wrong time.

I called one of my doctors, took her in, and we amputated more of her tail. She ended up with a bob tail. It looked hilarious, but she recovered fine. We had her for many years to come, and she was such a blessing.

Responsible for All

For many years than I care to remember, I thought I was responsible for helping all the lost-and-found, sick, abused, and homeless animals.

The first, was T-Bird, which was an earlier story. The next was Coallee. We had performed a spay on a very pregnant cat, and I could not bear to see the three full-term kittens euthanized. So three of us from the hospital took them. We knew it would be constant care, and my entire family would have to help, but we wanted to try.

Coallee was female and all black. We all took turns, feeding, cleaning. Watching her grow was amazing. I knew her chances were slim due to her not having her mother's milk. She did well for two weeks, and we even have home movies of her crawling around a ruler, so we could see how big she was. My kids were having a lot of fun with her as well.

Then suddenly one day, she would not eat and was listless. We took her into the hospital right away, and we tried giving her warm fluids and supportive care, but she passed away that night. Even more sad, the other two kittens did not survive either. A crushing blow to all of us, but we do have the memories of trying.

Next was Coal. Coal's owner brought her and her four sisters to be euthanized because they could not find homes. So once again, I took the all-black female. She was eight weeks old.

Coal was a fun cat and never did much to alarm us. However, she was possessed when we had the fireplace lit. She would actually lie underneath it (it was a free-standing fireplace). I could not imagine how hot it was, but she seemed perfectly content. When she would finally come out, you could barely touch her. She lived to be a ripe old eighteen years old!

Shortly after we got Coal, another adorable kitten was brought in. Someone found him along the road. Since I still thought it was my responsibility, I took him. He was a tan tiger and we named him "Rainbow" since there was one evident the day he came home. He was definitely one of our favorites. He would sit up and beg like a dog and would retrieve pieces of foil balls and bring them back to you and drop them and wanted you to throw them again and again. Such a cool cat.

Unfortunately, he had a skin condition and had to be on high doses of a drug that had complications. He developed a lung condition and needed surgery. I took him to a specialist in Maryland who tried, but Rainbow did not survive. I went back and got him and buried him under a tree in our back yard. We all missed him!

There were a few dogs I fostered, but just could not keep all of them. Frank was a lovable four-month-old German Shepherd whose owner did not want him because his ears would not stand! True! I took him for a few days until I found him a great home.

Next was Vanilla, a six-month-old mixed Lab whose owner no longer wanted him because he would not hunt! Again, true! I still have this great picture of Vanilla on a Sit 'n Spin with my daughter. He was a lovely dog, and I was able to place him with a good home as well.

Storm of the Year

It was to be the "storm of the year." It was a Friday, and the snow was to start early and a possible two to three feet was predicted. At this time, I was driving a 1972 Thunderbird that was huge, close to the ground, and did not go well in snow. I only lived a few miles from the practice, and the plan was to go in early, get everything done, and get out by lunchtime.

Snow started early and was coming down quickly. One owner and one associate had came in. We treated all the pets and saw a few emergencies. I remember the UPS man coming in and telling us to leave and how bad it was getting. The two doctors both had four-wheel drive and so I asked if I could leave around noon. They told me they were leaving to go skiing and instructed me to stay until the last client picked up some medication. When I asked who was going to come in and feed the pets in the kennel that afternoon, she told me she would come back.

So, I waited and waited.

At two, we had well over a foot of snow. I was really getting nervous. I called the client again and was told, "No way am I coming out in this mess." So I began my attempt to get out.

To get out of this parking area, you had to go up a hill. No way would my car make it. I tried and tried, shoveled areas around the wheels, and did everything I could, but no luck. It was snowing like crazy. Keep in mind there were no cells phones yet. I finally went back in and called my husband. He said he would take our daughters to the neighbors and come in to help. Keep in mind he was driving a van.

Quite a while later, he arrived and said they were closing the road we would normally travel, and we would have to try another road. By now I was soaked and freezing and just wanted to get home. It was now five, getting dark, and the owner never returned to feed the pets. I went back in, tried to call her, and she did not answer. I fed, walked, and medicated all the pets and out I went again.

I finally got out of the parking lot, went on the other road, and stopped at a gas station, as I was on E. There were cars stranded everywhere and still snowing hard. After getting gas, I went to start my car, and it would not start. After multiple attempts, my husband opened the hood, and the entire engine was packed with snow. Then we heard that the road we were going to try was being closed as well!

I broke down at this time and had no idea how we would get home. I went inside the gas station and called our neighbors, who assured us they could keep our girls. An older man also walked into the station and had heard about our dilemma and asked us where we lived. We told him, and he said he has a four-wheel drive, and he would try and get us home. I could not believe it.

So we left my car and my husband's van, and in the Jeep we went. You could not see anything; it was snowing so hard. It was now eight, and we had well over two feet of snow. After about an hour or so, he got us within a few blocks of our house and could go no further. We were so grateful; we told him we would walk the rest of the way. We thanked him and offered the few dollars we had on us, but he refused. We did trudge through two feet of snow for a few blocks and got home around ten, soaked to the bone, freezing, hungry, but oh, so grateful.

Next afternoon, we got a ride and went back to get our cars. We asked the owner of the station if he knew who the guy who helped us, and he said yes and told us his name. We looked him up, and we sent him a "huge" thank-you basket. It was truly "the storm of the year."

And on a footnote, when I called my boss and told her I would not be in the next day, her response was, "Oh, I had a great time skiing."

Really?

Special Owners

I n all the veterinary hospitals I have worked in, there are always those "special cat owners." This phrase meant they had an enormous number of cats, which creates challenges.

The very first one I met was Virginia Cross. She was a single older woman who lived with her mother in an old Victorian home in York. I so remember her car. It was an old Ford station wagon with wood paneling on the side and a nonexisting muffler system. When she turned it off, it always backfired with a thick puff of smoke. She would visit the practice often with a cat, usually with a urinary problem. Due to having so many cats with this problem, she would also pick up ten large bags of special cat food. When we loaded it in her car, we never knew what we would find when you lifted the hatch. Once there was a squirrel, which jumped out and scared me to death. Another time, there was a bag of trash smoldering, and the most memorable, finding a guy in the back, under a blanket. Apparently, Virginia had picked him up from the street, but again, she forgot to tell anyone!

Many times when she came in, she had the wrong cat or gave us the wrong name or remembered she took a new one in and forgot to name it.

There was a period of time when Virginia had gotten ill and asked me to come in and help her medicate some cats for a few days. The house on the outside was grand and had a beautiful garden out back. Once I entered, I felt like Tippi Hedren on *The Birds* movie, except with cats. Cats, cats, cats, everywhere. On every chair, table, TV, and once I entered the kitchen, it was the same. On the table, chairs, counters, and even the stove and refrigerator. It was more than eerie. Some scurried away, while most just sat and stared. A few hissed and looked quite ominous, but Virginia assured me they were all okay. I medicated who she pointed out to me, and some were a little tricky, but I got the job done and did this for several days.

Virginia and her mother were the dearest of ladies, and she has provided me with many great memories.

On the other end of the spectrum was Millie Heidlebaugh. A very wealthy older woman who drove an antique Mercedes. Always impeccably dressed in lovely suits, she owned forty cats. She would tell us how she fed all the cats' canned food on paper plates twice a day with the help of her two maids. She also provided them with spring water and gave them their medications and would document all of this as well as noting who ate and who did not. She provided excellent care and always had the right cat with the right name and never complained about any costs. She would always say "Her cats were her life," and her husband would never say a word!

Needless to say, she was amazing and so very special. I felt blessed knowing her. I told her, "If I die and come back as a cat, I want you to find me." This would make her laugh hysterically.

Country

Hands down, my experience with Country and his owner William Lovess were the most unique. Mr. Lovess was an older gentleman who owned a furniture store in Keytown. His dog was a huge wonderfully engaging yellow Lab. We did not meet until Country was an old dog with many problems. Mr. Lovess came for a second opinion as his original veterinarian said Country should be put to sleep. Mr. Lovess did not agree with this decision and said he would do *anything* to keep Country going, and money was not a concern.

After a full workup, we diagnosed Country with severe heart disease and major hip dysplasia. We developed a strict treatment plan with new doses of medication for both the heart and hips, and a new diet. It seemed Mr. Lovess fed Country everything he ate. Steak, seafood, you name it, Country ate it!

It was so obvious the connection between this dog and his owner. For several months, Country did better, and Mr. Lovess was so pleased that he provided all new furniture for the practice. Then Country had a cardiac crisis, and we were not sure he would survive. He required round-the-clock oxygen, and he begged us to stay with him. So Dr. Rossi and I remained by his side all night long, provided the oxygen, and gave lots of other medications, and lo and behold, Country rallied again and went home several days later.

It was at this point that Mr. Lovess approached me and asked if I would come to his home daily to check on Country. He wanted his vitals taken, check his heart and lungs, his hydration, and anything else needed. I could not say no. So for about three months, I traveled to his gorgeous home and assessed Country every day. He had his own room with a huge mattress and anything you could think of. We had a few scares, but the doctors continued to adjust his medications, and Country continued to stabilize.

There came a day where he was developing alot of fluid in his lungs, his heart was weakening, and overall condition deteriorating. Dreading it, I had to tell Mr. Lovess I thought we were nearing the end. Mr. Lovess just looked at me and said we were taking Country to the University of Pennsylvania for a heart transplant! And he was dead serious. He spoke to all the doctors, and they tried to explain that this procedure was not done on dogs, but Mr. Lovess was not having any of it.

So he asked me to go along with him, and we packed Country up, with an IV and oxygen, and left for Philadelphia.

Frankly, I was quite nervous the whole way fearing Country would die. But I learned a long time earlier, you should *never* say that to Mr. Lovess. I felt a huge sigh of relief when we arrived. After many specialists examined Country, we all met in a large conference room. Mr. Lovess just stared and asked, "When can you do the transplant?" You could have heard a pin drop! All the doctors tried to explain that all of Country's organs were failing, and nothing more could be done. Mr. Lovess then said he had a million dollars, and he wanted that heart transplant. Talk about a shock. No one said anything for a few seconds, but then, once again, they all stated this surgery is not possible, and even if they could, Country's other organs would not support the anesthesia. Mr. Lovess had tears streaming down his face as he pleaded and pleaded. After what seemed like an eternity, he just stood up and said, "Let's go." So we packed Country up again and came home. He never said one word the whole way home. As we got close, I asked if we were going back to the hospital or his home. He said the hospital, and we admitted Country again.

The next day, he met with all the doctors and said no matter what the cost, he wanted to keep Country alive. He just could not face the reality of the situation. The doctors told him he needed to make some serious decisions as they did not think Country would make it through the day. Sobbing, he said he would go get a casket as he wanted Country buried with him. A few hours later, Country passed away with Mr. Lovess by his side. The entire staff was a complete mess, and we all felt so bad but knew Country was in a better place.

Then things got even stranger. Mr. Lovess asked us to bathe Country, cut his nails, clean his ears, and brush him out as he wanted a viewing for his family and friends. Well, to remind you, you do not say no to Mr. Lovess, so we did as he requested. We prepared Country and placed him on a silk blanket, and his family and friends did arrive for the viewing. It was all so, so sad. He asked us to keep Country until the next day. Next morning, he came in, visibly shaken. He said he called *all* the cemeteries, and no one would bury Country beside him. Said he offered any amount of money, but still no luck. He said, no matter what, he would get Country buried with him.

A week went by, and still no one would do it. Stating he could not live without him by his side, he purchased a freezer, lined it with silk blankets, and you guessed it, transported Country into this and moved him back in his house.

We remained close friends for many years, and when Mr. Lovess died, no one ever said anything, but I *know* he and Country are together.

They Will Eat the Strangest Things

I 've learned never to say never in the world of veterinary medicine. It does not cease to amaze me what animals will eat and why.

This is the story of Georgia, a middle-aged Beagle and just a lovely dog. It all started when the owners went on vacation and had a neighbor coming in to take care of Georgia. The dog had stopped eating, seemed sad, and the neighbor just thought Georgia was missing her owners.

The owners returned and knew immediately something was wrong and rushed her in. She came in, not able to walk, head hung down, and a very painful belly. We took some x-rays and wow, lots of different sizes of round objects. It seemed Georgia ate a change purse and all the change! The contents of certain coins are very toxic and are extremely dangerous. Knowing the coins had been there for several days was quite alarming.

Our plan of attack was to do an exploratory and get the coins out and then try and treat the toxicity. The owners were told she may not make it, but they wanted to try. Georgia was anesthetized, and the doctor found six quarters, four dimes, six nickels, and four pennies. I remember calling York Hospital as the medicine needed was of the human form, and they were so interested in the case and sold us the drug. It was touch and go for a few days, but by golly, Georgia made it!

Of course, when we discharged her, she had incurred a very large bill. I brought out he baggie with the $2.24 in it and asked if they wanted to apply it to the bill. We all laughed, but they said they were going to frame these coins as a "memory of their vacation"!

On the same story line, I met dear Mr. Edwards, a short bald eighty-year-old single man who owned a little white Maltese named Angel. He told us Angel had a history of eating things and felt this was her problem.

Again, we took x-rays, and there was definitely something blocking her intestines but could not make out what it was. So in goes the doctor again, and we're all waiting to find out what she ate. As Dr. Perkins pulled it out, we could see it was red in color. Upon further examination, it was a woman's red thong! There was a lot of laughter in that surgery room. We finished the surgery and felt Angel should be fine.

When Mr. Edwards called about Angel, Dr. Perkins told him we found the blockage and removed it. Mr. Edwards was insistent on knowing exactly what it was, and Dr. Perkins told him. There was dead silence on the phone.

Luckily, Angel did fine and went home two days later. When Mr. Edwards arrived to pick her up, we went over her post-op instructions and asked if he had any questions. He then bashfully asked, "Please do not tell my daughter, she'll kill me!"

This story is over twenty-five years old, so I think I'm safe in telling now!

All the Ways Clients Respond When Asked "How Old Is Your Pet?"

Well, Sally was just starting to walk!

Well, we lived on the farm and it was planting time!

Well, I had just divorced my second man!

Well, it was really cold and snowy, and the Super Bowl was on and the Packers played!

Well, I was in college, and my boyfriend was Tom at the time!

Well, I had one kid, was pregnant with the second kid, well no, I had two kids and got pregnant with the third. Well, no, it seemed I was always pregnant there for a while!

Well, the shelter said he was one, but I thought he was two or three, and my dad said he was five when we got him!

Well, found her as a stray. That was ten years ago, so she may be ten to twenty years old!

Well, Susie was a baby, and she's now thirty!

Well, it was a hot summer!

Well, I was just a kid, my mom and dad were away, and my brother found the cat!

Well, you get the picture!

A Cake to Remember

During the years I worked at one particular practice, we had a fun routine of getting all the staff a birthday cake on their special day. And we were always being inventive on what to put on the cake. The bakery we used at the time was so accommodating in meeting our requests.

There were many cakes that stick out in my mind, but one in particular was made for Lucy, a receptionist, who was getting married. I had asked for the bakers to try and make a picture of a negligee. "Sure, we'll try," they said.

Now I always picked up the cakes and put them on a side step, then came in and went around getting in so Lucy could not see it and we could surprise her. The bakers had done a wonderful job, and it was perfect!

To give you a perspective of how the practice was built, there was a house right beside it, with a small fence and walkway in between. One of our associates lived in this house. He had a German Shepherd at the time named Sadie.

When I got inside, I went straight to the side door to get the cake. I opened the door, and Sadie had been let out and had her face right in the middle of the cake, chowing down! I screamed in surprise, and all the staff came running. All we could do was laugh. Of course, we got Sadie away from the cake and brought it in to examine. She did quite a number on the cake, and all that was left of the negligee was the top part!

You know what's even worse? We cut around the part Sadie ate and still had the cake.

Veterinary staff does not hold back when it comes to food!

Anything but Normal

It was supposed to be a normal day, and my job that day was to be in surgery. We had a full schedule, and everything was going beautifully. Our next surgery was to be a spay on a new patient, a lovely cocker named Jem. Part of my job was to shave, perform a surgical scrub, and move her into surgery. Dr. Summers sedated her, we intubated, and Dr. Summers went to scrub.

I turned her over and began to clip the abdominal area. I looked and looked, and I could not believe my eyes. She had a penis coming out of her vulva! I quickly called Dr. Summers, and she came running. She saw what I saw, and her mouth dropped as well. She examined Jem more thoroughly and sure enough, she had both male and female parts. We quickly took her off of anesthesia, and Dr. Summers called the owner.

Since this was extremely rare, the dog was sent to the University of Pennsylvania to perform the surgery, and she was considered a hermaphrodite and had an entire two sets of reproductive parts, one male and one female. All the male parts, except the penis, were in her abdomen.

Jem did well after surgery, and when we saw her for a suture removal appointment, the owners remarked they never noticed anything before, but always knew she was a "Jem."

The one and only time I have ever seen this in a pet! Really cool case.

Oh, What a Relief It Is!

I have had the pleasure of hiring and working with many relief doctors over the years. These are doctors that fill in while owners/associates cannot work. They are usually very hardworking people, but also very interesting.

The first one I hired was Lois Burkins. She was an engaging, lovely lady who had traveled all over the world with her husband. She would hold us in a trance at lunch (when we got a lunch), describing her travels and all the different ethnic groups she came in contact with. She had planned a trip to Africa and brought me back a wooden giraffe, which I still treasure to this day.

Lois was a very good doctor but had a constant requirement for us to do a CBC on just about every pet before she treated it. A CBC is a complete blood count and back in these days, there were no machines to do this procedure, and you had to do this all by hand. So we all got used to drawing blood before we sent her to see the pet just to keep up. All the technicians got quite proficient after working with Lois, and she was not only a good doctor but also a great storyteller.

The first guy I ever hired was Luke Wagner. Luke was a physical fitness guru who also had traveled extensively. He was really into hiking, surfing, and had even climbed Mt. Kilimanjaro! His free and easygoing spirit was evident as he would arrive for each shift wearing a colorful Hawaiian shirt.

It took a little doing, but we did get him to wear a white coat to see patients, but he would not take off the Hawaiian shirt. His trait was to always get on the floor with every patient. It didn't matter if it was a big dog, little dog, nice cat, or not-so-nice cat. And clients loved it!

Again, a great doctor with a colorful personality.

And now, to the third and most memorable, Ariel Barak.

I first hired Dr. Barak when I was managing a practice in Hoovertown. Now you need to know, Hoovertown was a small conservative town. Ariel was from Israel and had a thick accent. I was not sure how the clients would accept him, but his credentials and references were quite good, so I decided to give it a try.

The first few shifts he worked, I or another staff member would stay in the room in case they could not understand him or have questions. And, yes, many clients had difficulty, and we would just repeat what he said, and things progressed just fine. Being an excellent doctor plus an excellent surgeon helped the transition, and I actually hired him also as a relief doctor at the emergency clinic I was managing as well.

Ariel did not speak much about his personal life until one unique weekend in June. One of my doctors had a family emergency and had to go out of town with a short notice and could not work the weekend. I called Ariel and luckily he agreed to work. One of my responsibilities was to make sure all these doctors had places to stay while working since many of them had very long commutes. The problem was there were no motels anywhere that weekend as there was a huge car show going on, and there was nothing available from Harrisburg to Lancaster.

I talked to my husband, and we decided to have him stay with us. Now I had never done this before, but felt it was the best option for everyone. I think all of us felt a little awkward, but Ariel finally agreed.

It was over the weekend that he opened up about his family in Israel, all the war and violence he witnessed, and what he saw as a child. It broke my heart to hear of his troubled past, but I expressed my respect and, of course, admiration for the man he had become.

We became very good friends, and he worked for me for many years before opening his own practice near Garrett. I still have the bottle of wine he gave me as a gift from that weekend. The wine was sent from Israel, and the bottle, the writing, and memory hold a special place in my heart.

Jerry, the Cat Guy

When I think of clients that have a lot of cats, I usually think of women. However, there was one guy, named Jerry, that sticks out as very special.

Jerry was a single, retired, older man who lived in a large house on the outskirts of Hoovertown. He had a lot of cats (no one ever really knew how many he had), but always knew who he brought in. Along with seeing his cats, Jerry was visiting us several times a week, and at least once a week, he would bring us a gallon of ice cream from a local homemade store. What a wonderful treat for all of us! Along with the ice cream, he would also bring antiques he would find, or just some knickknacks he would see and think we would like. Everyone in Hoovertown knew Perry, and we all loved him.

Trouble was, we soon could not keep up with eating all the ice cream, and there was no more room in our freezer! Of course, I was elected to have to tell him, and I suggested that he give some ice cream to the other businesses he visited regularly, so they all could enjoy the treats. He took the suggestion fine, and we all let a loud whew.

Jerry drove a rust-colored 1972 Rambler that was in cherry condition. It was his pride and joy, next to his cats. He never married, and we would kid him about fixing him up, and he would blush and say that "no woman could ever live with his cats." Jerry was a large man and had the kind of hair that he would sweep from side to side and always took pride in himself, his car, and most important, his cats.

Jerry lived to be a ripe old age, and I smile when I think about him.

Savage and the Wheels

This story is one from the parvo era. Gary was a young local
mechanic that had a guard dog named Savage. His name fit
him well. Savage was a very large, unneutered Rottweiler, and Gary
was the only one who could handle him. With him, he was just a big
baby, but without Gary, he would and could have really hurt you.

Now Gary had always had some financial issues and had owed
our clinic some money for a long time. We always thought he was a
hard worker, just not good with saving any money.

Guess who came down with parvo? You guessed it, Savage. And
what a case it was. He brought him in and actually had to try and
carry him; he was that sick. Extreme vomiting and bloody diarrhea
and close to death. We immediately put an IV in him, while Gary
held, as Savage, as sick as he was, still wanted to hurt us. All the parvo
cases were kept in our isolation ward, and the plan was for Gary to
have to come in three to four times a day to help us, so we could
treat Savage.

Of course, he wanted an estimate of costs and seeing how sick
he was, we knew it was going to be a large bill, and we did not
even know if he would make it. Again, I was the person to deal with
these issues, and I was very honest with Gary. He still owed us from
some last visits, and with this estimate, it was well over one thousand
dollars. Of course, he broke down as this dog was his life.

So we started to talk about how to get some funds, and I
remember sitting on the front porch of the practice with him after a

treatment, and I saw what he drove: a fancy van with murals on the sides and very fancy wheels. I said, "Hey, how about selling those wheels? They would fetch a pretty price in York." He just looked and looked at me and fell silent. He then started to smile and said, "Gosh, darn it, I'll try anything to save Savage."

And you know what, Savage did make it, but it was a long haul, and Gary did indeed sell the wheels and paid the practice all that was owed. From that point on, he never had fancy wheels again but paid his bills on time.

A valuable lesson learned!

Oh, the Colorful Folks I Did Not Hire

There have been many colorful characters I interviewed, and here are just a few.

First, there was Bobbi Jo. She was a large lady who wore pink spandex pants and matching shirt for her interview. To match her outfit, she wore, of course, pink flip-flops. Oh, we're not done.

She had a purse that looked just like a skunk and blew bubbles with her Bubble Yum gum the whole time!

Next, was Sandy. Sandy was in her early twenties and brought her two children with her. Her son was two and her daughter was three. They must've been playing in the mud before they came, and she did not seem to care. They both had lollipops, and you could not make out what flavor, all was covered in mud.

Now I truly understand if a mother does not have child care; however, these children appeared to be on a sugar high, and she could not control them in any way. I honestly could not get any information from her due to the children, and she ended by standing up, yelling at them at the top of her lungs, and said to me, "Don't worry, I wouldn't hire me either. I stink."

I was interviewing for a veterinary technician position, and a man applied. We don't get many guys to apply, so I was intrigued. In walked Mark, a man in his twenties and seemed pleasant. I first asked him about his experience, and he politely remarked how he had worked on Chevys, Fords, Buicks, Cadillacs, and trucks of all types. I had to chuckle. I stated this was a veterinary position, not a mechanical position. Bashfully, he replied, "Gosh, I thought it meant you work on veterans cars?" Let's just say, that interview ended quickly.

And last, but not least, Juanita. She had applied for an animal care attendant. She was an older woman with a thick foreign accent. She had a resume, which stated she had been a nanny most of her life. When I asked why she applied for this position, I thought she said, "To take care of the babies." When I explained the position, she kept saying the same thing over and over. She did not understand me, and I did not understand her. After what seemed forever, I decided to write it down for her. She looked at the paper and said, "I no read." I asked her how she made her resume if she could not read, and she said, "I found it." Another interview ended quickly.

A Student's Worst Nightmare

Having students come into a practice to observe or intern for a few weeks had always been rewarding for me. I so enjoyed their enthusiasm, and many of my students had gone on to be veterinarians. Seventeen to be exact so far.

Many years ago, I had such a student who was interning, and her name was Cheryl. Cheryl was in her first year of prevet and was with us for six weeks over the summer. Most of the students just wanted to jump in and observe surgery, and Cheryl was no different. However, I had strict guidelines as to what they would learn or be exposed to and a timeline for the training.

After three weeks into her training, she was permitted to observe from the door how we sedated, intubated, and scrubbed the pet prior to surgery. I would always watch closely to see their reaction and to make sure they could handle it. Cheryl handled this well.

In the fourth week, if everything is going as planned, they were allowed to be in the surgery room, with the proper attire, and watch the surgery. But my message was always the same: if you are not feeling well, getting faint, or anything else, get out of the surgery room and fast! Many times this came on quickly for the inexperienced.

Cheryl had watched two surgeries that fateful morning and had done fine. We had a large shepherd on the table being spayed. We were all talking and all was going well when she just stopped talking. One moment later, she fainted and fell right on the instrument tray and sent all the instruments flying. On the way down, she also knocked the surgery table, and the dog fell on the floor. We all yelled, and while we were worried about both Cheryl and the dog, the doctor and I worked on the dog and two other staff members came to get Cheryl. We got the dog back on the table and immediately began to flush out everything thoroughly with sterile fluids. I have to admit, it was a bit scary for a while as the tube had come out of the dog's mouth and she had started to wake and the incision was not closed yet.

Meanwhile, they got Cheryl up and out to the treatment room and applied ice to her head and cheek and eye. Luckily, she was okay, except for her bruised face and ego. She was so embarrassed and said she had no warning, she just went down and down hard!

We were so grateful both Cheryl and our patient were fine, but from then on, *no one* got in our surgery room. They had to remain outside and look in!

And Justice for All

How often do you see dogs walking their owners? The dog is pulling and pulling, and it does not look pleasant for either party. For many years, I got interested in helping both these dogs and their owners and make their walks enjoyable. I used training methods with a product called the Gentle Leader. It never failed me. I would ask the owner to purchase the Gentle Leader, and I would give them one hour of my time (at no charge). But I also told them I will not stop training until they get the dog they want. It gave me such satisfaction to see the dog when we started and the amazing results when we were finished. There are a few dogs that stand out in my mind, but hands down, Justice wins as the ultimate!

I met Justice and his owners when he was about four months old. He was a black Lab, and the owners brought him in for vaccines, but were also concerned about his behavior. He *never* stopped jumping. After the doctor saw him, she came to me and asked if I would look at him and possibly help train him. I walked in the exam room, and he literally jumped so high he hit the ceiling! And he really never did stop. Up and down he went, the owners yelling more and more, which did nothing. I then grabbed his leash, and instead of pulling up, I gave a short tug downward, and he suddenly stopped. I gave a quick summary of how I could help, and they jumped (ha!) at the chance. He was a really sweet puppy, just completely out of control.

We scheduled a session the next day. The mister brought Justice, and off we went out back. Just fitting the Gentle Leader took some time, but we finally had it on, and the first command was to get them to sit and stay. After about ten minutes, he was sitting like a pro. Then the big issue, getting him to heal and walk without jumping. I was constant and persistent in my commands and my downward tugs. He reared like a horse over and over and over for about fifty minutes. Never stopping, he finally gave up and just sat. We were all so overjoyed! My staff was also utilized as distractions, so the dogs could get used to walking around them. They all did a wonderful job and really enjoyed seeing the results.

Justice's first hour ended up being two because of his high energy and his ADD. I firmly believe all puppies have it; some just have more than others. I gave the mister homework to do, and he was to work with Justice at least a half hour every day for two weeks and usually, the dog responded nicely.

When I called to check on their progress, the mister said he was terrible and still going nuts in the house, tearing everything up and jumping. I said I would see him again.

Next day, I took Justice out back, placed the Gentle Leader on him, and we had to go over everything again. Again, he was completely out of control, and I was quite perplexed. I went over to his owner and questioned how he was training at home. He then replied, "Never did any, he's too much for us, just want you to take him and finish." I could not believe it!

So we had a long conversation, and I tried to explain that Justice was *his* dog, and I would certainly help, but the dog lived with them and needed to learn from him and his wife. He kept shaking his head and said he couldn't do it. I agreed to work with Justice as long as it took, but oh my, it took a very, very long time.

Each week, I had to start over since the dog was not being worked with in between. And jump, my gosh, could this dog jump! And he was getting bigger and bigger. Many of these days I would come in, looking a bit haggard, as he would have torn some clothes or just had me hairy and dirty from jumping on me until he remembered some training.

When he was six months old, we had recommended getting him neutered. Again, we got a negative response. They were *never* going to neuter Justice! And he got bigger and bigger and stronger and stronger.

When Justice was about seven months, his owners requested him to be boarded for two weeks while they moved. No problem, and I continued to work with him while he was with us. The problem was the owners did not come back for him after the two weeks. I kept calling and leaving messages, and finally two weeks later, they called back and said they were evicted from their house and were too embarrassed to tell us. Their goal was to get him in about two more weeks.

The weeks came and went and after three months and many calls and many excuses for not picking him up, they actually came to see him. They did not recognize him. He was so well behaved, listened, and was so happy. We talked about trying to find him another home as we did not feel it was best to keep him kenneled, but again, they said no.

It was close to Christmas and the mister called to say they had gotten back into their home and were coming to get him. We were all so elated!

We bathed him, made him so handsome, and told him he was going home. They arrived and, indeed, took him home, and I said a little prayer for them all.

Justice took literally everything I had to train him, but again, the method still has never failed!

I Thought It Was Just a Song

A few years after becoming a technician, a new test was developed to diagnose feline leukemia. It first involved taking a blood sample from the cat and mixing it with several solutions.

Snuffles was a gorgeous blue-point Himalayan kitten that was eight weeks old. I was restraining the kitten while Dr. Summers took the blood. As she finished, the kitten turned around and scratched me on my left wrist. No big deal, happened a lot. I cleaned it well, and we moved on. Luckily, Snuffles was negative for leukemia.

After two weeks, this scratch was just not healing, and I thought it was odd. Along with this, I was not feeling well overall, and my lymph nodes were enlarged on my left side, and I also had a low-grade fever.

We were standing in the treatment room and were all talking and several staff remarked how bad I looked. I mentioned all my symptoms, and Dr. Pitney looked up and said, "Julie, I think you have cat scratch fever." Well, everyone, including me, just laughed and started to sing the song. She stopped us and said, "No, it's really a serious disease." She made me call my doctor immediately.

The receptionist asked me what was going on, and I told her I thought I had cat scratch fever. She also laughed out loud and started to sing the song and said, "You must be joking." I assured her I was not, and then she said, "I thought it was just a song."

I got an appointment later that day, and the nurse had the same reaction. She laughed, joked, and sang the song. But as she wrote all my symptoms down, she verified the fever, nonhealing scratch, and enlarged lymph nodes, but I think she still thought I was crazy!

In walked Dr. Myes with two male residents. He asked if they could stay, and I said sure. As he read my chart, he relayed the findings first to the residents, and once again, they both laughed and sang the song. He quickly stopped them, looked at them with a serious demeanor, and said, "She's probably right. Cat scratch fever is real and quite serious."

After examining me, he walked over to his enormous bookshelves and pulled out a book and told them to do some research and to figure out what to do. The residents dove into the book, and when they found the information, it was like they found gold! They told me the virus comes from certain cats that have a specific herpes virus and only shed that virus at varying times. If all these factors happen together, the cat can infect a person. The treatment is a specific antibiotic for three weeks and sometimes an IV antibiotic is needed as well.

After the appointment, the residents, the nurses, and receptionists all apologized. I replied, "No problem, I thought it was just a song too."

After three weeks on the antibiotics, I was back to normal!

Believe me, cat scratch fever is *not* just a song.

Mazie

Helping a doctor perform a C-section was usually a fun plus rewarding experience. Taking the pups, cleaning them, helping them to breathe, and treating them if they had problems were all a part of it.

I met Mazie, a very large Mastiff when she was three years old. She needed a C-section, was a delight to work with, and we delivered thirteen healthy puppies, and all was good.

A year later, same thing occurred. Mazie was now four, weighed a whopping 180 pounds, and her owner decided this would be her last litter.

Due to her weight and not to have to carry her far, we had her in our surgery prep area, just hanging out with me. This room was not large, just had a sink, small counter, which housed the autoclave, and an area to wrap our surgical packs. It was tight quarters with Mazie lying against the door.

Dr. Pitney was getting her anesthesia drugs together out in the treatment room. I had surgery all prepared and turned around to get Mazie up, and she growled and raised her lips. I was completely shocked as she had never acted like this before. I tried talking to her, and then she stood up and looked like she was going to charge at me! As Dr. Pitney tried to open the door, Mazie was tight against it and would not budge.

I was trapped, and Mazie was going nowhere. I yelled out and let her know what was happening. I tried to remain calm and just kept talking, but she was having none of it. After half an hour, my Mastiff was getting more agitated, so I stopped trying and told Dr. Pitney to get her owner here and fast!

Another hour passed, Mazie layed down but was still blocking the door. She never took her eyes off of me. Her owner arrived and talked to her through the door. Mazie immediately stood, and as she stood, her owner pushed the door open a crack. She bravely put her hand through the door, and Mazie sniffed her. Her total attitude changed, and tail wagging, we left the door open, and they were reunited in the hallway.

We then decided to have her owner hold her head while we gave her a sedative. A short time later, we could anesthetize her and got her into surgery. Unfortunately, she only delivered three live puppies, and perhaps she knew.

As soon as she woke up, she was growling again, so her owner came and took her and the puppies home.

We all loved Mazie, but were all glad this was her last litter!

A Complete 180

B reeders seem to be known as either "good" or "bad."

In one practice, we had a breeder of Cane Corsos and Rottweilers, and he had a definite "bad" reputation. Most of his dogs were nasty, and he wanted them that way. He even had the reputation of selling dogs to be guard dogs or even fighting dogs, although it was never proven.

He visited us often, always with sickly puppies, and unhealthy breeding dogs. He had his own poor vaccine protocols but would never listen to the doctor's advice. His brash and all-knowing attitude was hard to take with every visit. All he wanted was medication. It was a particular hard year when he lost several litters to parvovirus and some unknown diseases, and it was really hurting his pocketbook that this story begins.

He came in angry and questioning why this was happening. I have to admit, the doctors were all frustrated with him as they had spent so much time with him to no avail. They asked me to try and work with him one final time.

I met with Mr. King and said I really wanted him to be successful, and the place to start would be to see his kennel. He warily agreed, and the next day, I drove out to his home. He lived in an old farmhouse with a large run-down barn out back. That was the kennel.

Beware of Dog signs were everywhere, and he told me to honk my horn when I arrived, but to stay in my car. Wow! I saw why quickly.

Six large dogs, three Corsos and three Rotties came running to my car and looked vicious. All I could think about was the woman in the car in the *Cujo* movie!

Mr. King came out, called the dogs, put them in the house, and said it was okay to get out.

We walked to the barn, went inside, and the stench almost knocked me over. I had to cover my nose and mouth, but I said nothing. It was dark, but once he turned the lights on, I could see that with each old horse stall were now dogs, with a small amount of hay. I asked him what his cleaning protocols were, what cleaners he used, what food he fed, and what records he kept. He looked stunned at my questions and replied, "They get fed Big Red, and stalls are cleaned with water weekly, and I can remember what I do with each dog." *Unbelievable*, I thought.

The dogs all looked unhealthy, thin, dull coats, and many rushed to the front of the stalls, snarling. What had I gotten myself into?

He had about twenty dogs at the time; half were Corsos and half Rotties. He had one litter of five puppies, and they all looked terrible. I could not stand to be in that barn any longer due to the smell.

As we exited, I told him he had *a lot* of work to do, but was he really prepared to do it? He said, "Yes, as long as you help me." And I agreed, as long as he promised to see this through.

This started one of the biggest challenges of my career. I first consulted with the doctors, so we were all in agreement on how to proceed. The primary job was cleaning the place and getting some natural lighting and good nutrition to all the dogs. Second would be to get them all vaccinated and wormed correctly and keep records.

I met with Mr. King, and we set up our plan of action. He knew he was going to have to spend money to make money, but more importantly, have healthier, happier dogs.

We first virtually gutted the barn and had chain-link kennels installed with cement floors and gutters in front. Then we had windows placed for natural lighting and ventilation and purchased heaters for the winter. We added the proper disinfectants and introduced a high-quality food.

As each phase started, he grumbled about the money he was spending, and several times I thought he was going to bail on me, but I kept reminding him the promise he made.

I could now visit the barn, and the stench was gone. The dogs looked so much better, and many of them were no longer lunging and snarling. I now believe those dogs were truly not mean, just ill.

Many still had diarrhea, so we ramped up our worming and vaccine protocol, and I taught him how to keep simple but complete records.

After a month passed and all the dogs were wormed, he still had the diarrhea issues and he was now becoming angry. He came into the office and really yelled at me and blamed me for the problem. I told him I won't stop until we figure it out. I then met with the doctors again, and we were all still perplexed.

We decided I would visit the farm again. This time, only one guard dog arrived. He still looked scary, but now had a shiny coat with good weight. I entered the barn and was quite satisfied with our results. All the dogs looked healthy, kennels were clean, and records updated. Mr. King and I talked for quite a while to see if I could figure out a common denominator with all the dogs. As his helper came in to clean, do the morning feeding and change the water, it hit me. Water!

I was sure Mr. King had a well, and indeed he did. I asked him when he had the water tested, and he said never. We had it tested immediately, and it was saturated with *E. coli* and several other parasites. We treated the water, and within two weeks, all diarrhea issues resolved. Hallelujah!

He wanted to try a breeding of his Rotties, and we all held our breaths. No problems, and nine healthy puppies were born. He came to the office and shared pictures and beamed like a new father. His demeanor had softened, and he actually smiled and was pleasant.

He then gave me a thank-you card, and in it was a gift certificate to a local restaurant. As he walked away, he tipped his hat and said, "Julie, you earned it!"

A Trucker Gone Mad

As I have written several stories about parvo, this is one that has a different twist.

Ginny Anderson brought in a ten-week-old lemon-colored beagle named Poppy. Poppy had had no vaccines and had contracted the parvovirus. She was very ill, and we were unsure if she could survive. Ginny told us to do everything we could.

Several days passed, and Poppy was not much better. Dr. Perkins even called Ginny to see if she wanted to continue treatment or gave her the option of euthanasia. Ginny authorized us to continue.

It was a Tuesday, and Poppy had been with us for seven days. We felt she had finally "turned the corner," but was still very weak.

This practice was located on a small side street. That Tuesday afternoon, we heard a loud truck noise and saw an eighteen-wheeler pull up. It took up virtually the entire block.

In walked a big burly man who demanded to see the doctor. Of course, none were present at the time, so I came out to see him. He said he was Mr. Anderson, and he wanted his pup and now! I escorted him into an exam room. He looked completely exhausted, with reddened big bags under his eyes, and it appeared he had not slept or showered in days. I started to tell him about Poppy's condition. He immediately interrupted me, and told me, "Just shut up, and get my dog." Then he pulled a small handgun from his coat. I said, "Whoa, wait a minute. Put that away." (I know now how wrong I was.)

I then agreed to get his dog and went and got Poppy. I had to put the entire isolation garb on and left her hooked to her IV, and out we came. My staff just stood there and gasped. First, I put newspaper on the exam table and laid her down. He was in a state of shock when he saw her. He spoke to her in baby talk and asked if he could pet her. I replied yes. As he stroked her back, she did raise her head a bit and licked his hand. It was as if a lightbulb went off. He completely changed, kept apologizing, and cried like a baby.

I then explained what she had and that she was better, but not ready to go home yet. Mr. Anderson said he had been driving across the country for over a week and had not slept or stopped in three days. His wife just told him Poppy could not come home and no details were shared. All of us felt it was more of sleep deprivation that caused his reaction than anything else.

After a short visit, I took her back to isolation, took off my garb, and went back into the exam room. Mr. Anderson was now on the bench sobbing again and apologizing. I reassured him all was okay and forgiven only if he promised to go home and get some rest. He agreed with no protest.

When he left, my entire staff said they had heard everything and were ready to call the police, and they all said I was crazy. I guess I was!

Three days later, Poppy was well enough to go home. Both Mr. and Mrs. Anderson came and brought along a big cake for the entire staff for pulling her through. The cake had an eighteen-wheeler on it, and it said, "Thank you all, and I'm sorry"!

Glad we all had a happy ending.

Bosses

I have been quite fortunate to have worked for some fine doctors over the years. For over twenty years, the veterinarians were not only the doctor, but the boss as well. No one had any managers; we all just did our jobs. In my opinion, a good boss challenges you, teaches you, lets you know what is expected of you, and rewards you for a good job.

However, there were a few who broke that mold. When you walk in to start your shift and say "Good Morning" and see a grouchy face, no smile, and no response, you knew it was not going to be a good day. Now everyone has a bad day, but when this behavior was consistent, it does affect everyone. The same applies when there is a lot of cursing, calling clients unkind names, throwing instruments during surgery, and showing a genuine lack of respect for the total team.

While I was a manager and would see this behavior, I would try and help these doctors see how destructive this was. Sometimes I would be successful, sometimes not. Knowing how important it is to treat your clients well all the time, I would try and point out in a professional way, how this was affecting the practice. My style of management was very hands on, and my door was always open to my staff. They would come and tell me things that these doctors would do and how it affected them. We all tried to share ways to help, but I must admit, there were several that I could not help.

In management, there should also be support of each other, as well as a mutual respect. I have always had the highest regard for veterinarians, as they work so hard, work long hours, perform many, many jobs, handle dangerous animals, and get dirty in the process. But one important fact these few doctors missed: staff do the same thing. They work long hours, perform lots of duties, and still get dirty.

One such sad memory of this behavior happened while we were preparing for a hurricane. We had two days' notice. The generators were started and prepared, gas was purchased, extension cords were ready, and a plan of action for both staff and the animals was all set. The storm came, and it was fierce, but we were fortunate not to have any major structural damage. However, the power was out, and it was to be out for at least two days. A skeleton staff arrived and got all the pets taken care of, and we decided we could see anyone who walked in the front exam room that had a window. And we did have clients arrive, some with sick or injured pets. I actually thought things were going pretty well, under the circumstances, and we were so proud of our hard work.

But all these doctors could do was argue on how to see the pets, how to collect payment, etc. They had lost sight of all the good the staff had done, and it ended up that most of the staff wanted to leave, and I could not blame them. I let them go, and I stayed all day, but it was a very long day!

I'll let you be the judge.

Flipper

As with many of my memories, there were so many colorful characters I have met.

One such lady was Kathy. She was a very large lady who rode a Harley and had eight tiny dogs. With every visit, Kathy would have two or three of her dogs in a backpack with her on the Harley, and I remember just seeing their little heads popping out of the pack. Hilarious! They were a combination of Chihuahua, Pomeranian, Teacup Poodle, and the rest were just mixed breeds. Kathy visited us often and would love to share her Harley and beach stories.

They were her two most favorite things in life. And she was not shy about telling you anything. I remember the day she came in and said she had something to show me. She pulled her shirt down, and she had gotten several large tattoos of dolphins on her shoulder and top of chest. They were quite colorful, and she said they were her Flippers. *Wow*, I thought!

It was a long time until we saw her again, and we often remarked how we missed her and her stories.

Then, as if she heard us, she walked in. We did not recognize her. She had gotten gastric bypass surgery and had lost over one hundred pounds! She really looked great, and she still had her big smile. She told us blow by blow how they did the surgery and that she had something else to show us. She was laughing as she again pulled her shirt down and said, "Look where Flipper has gone." It seemed that her dolphins had sagged with her weight loss and now hung down at her waist, and you could only see a small portion of them. She said they had left the ocean and went into a cave. Well, we all rolled and could not stop laughing. Kathy had the best sense of humor, and I will never forget her or her dolphins!

Julie's Taxi Service

Many of my friends had pets, and they were very confident in the doctors I worked for, and therefore, were clients. To tell you the truth, I can't remember when this all started, but I provided a taxi service for my friends' pets. They may have needed vaccines or were not feeling well, but for any reason, they would call me, and I would either pick them up or they would be at my house. For whatever reason, they all traveled well with me and for many years, I worked in a practice where I was on the road for an hour each way.

There were two in particular that were with me for many, many miles. The first being a barn cat named Comet. Comet was a sweet tan tiger cat, who just kept getting beat up on from other cats. Abscesses, wounds, you name it, that cat went through it. We would place him in a carrier, and he would scream and carry on the entire trip. He would also decide to "cut loose" with pooping and peeing, and so it was a normal routine to have to bathe him as well when we got to the hospital. It wasn't until we road together for about two years that he finally stopped. I guess he finally figured it out.

The second case was with a dear tiny Yorkie named Nosey. My friends, Ralph and Marge, had been taking her elsewhere for a while when they called and told me about some disturbing news. It seemed Nosey had a liver issue, and their doctor told them there was nothing else to be done and even recommended euthanasia.

Now Nosey was young, and when I heard the news, I asked if my doctors could take a look at her. They collected all her records, and

I took her in. From the moment she got in my car, she immediately jumped on my shoulder. Now, I was not comfortable with this, but in no way was she going to sit on the seat. So I drove with her thinking I would get a carrier on the trip home.

My doctors examined Nosey and her lab work and records. Yes, she did indeed have a liver issue, but we felt we could try and manage her with quite a few medications and regular blood draws to monitor her condition. After Ralph and Marge spoke to the docs, we all agreed to proceed.

On our first trip home together, I placed her in a carrier. She went absolutely bonkers and with her condition, I took her out. Up on my shoulder she went! She never moved and would just give me kisses the whole way. Now I know I should not have left this go on, but I did.

And we traveled for many years together, and I am so sad but proud to report that Nosey just recently passed away, and she would have been twenty years old in December of this year! What a testament to both the doctors and Ralph and Marge for giving her a wonderful life!

There were many pets my taxi service helped out. Parsley, Tickles, Paisley, Jazzie, Mocha, Bubbles, Cupid, Pepper, Hank, and Whitney are just a few names of the great pets I traveled with.

It Was a Sign

How many times have you passed a car and saw the dog had its head sticking out? These dogs generally look happy, with their tongues out and hair blowing in the wind, right? Well, I used to feel the same way, not so much anymore.

It was a crazy Monday morning, and we were full with appointments and surgery. The entire staff was running around with a furious pace. All of a sudden, a woman ran in the door and said her Lab had been in an accident and she needed help. Another technician and I ran out to the car. What I saw I will never forget!

Duke was a very large chocolate Lab, with an enormous block head and was a wonderful, engaging dog. It seems he had his head out the window the entire way, and the car must have been very close to the side of the road, and his head hit a sign. There was more blood everywhere than I had ever seen before. The dog was totally unconscious, and honestly, we thought he was gone. But I did get a heartbeat, so we rushed him in, blood spurting from all areas of his head, face, and neck area. We covered him with a blanket, and the doctor slowly removed it inch by inch and tied off the vessels the best we could. While he was doing this, I placed an IV catheter in his back leg, and we administered fluids and medications at a very fast rate. Everyone involved was covered in blood, and our waiting room looked like a disaster had occurred.

We asked any routine appointments if they would reschedule, and of course, all the clients agreed. They couldn't get out of the office fast enough. Then the receptionists called and tried to reschedule upcoming appointments as we knew we would be with this dog for a long time.

No one said anything, but we all thought Duke would not make it. But we just kept tying off bleeders and his heart kept going. He had lost an eye, most of his teeth were gone or just hanging, and it was just awful to see.

Once we got the bleeding under control, the doctors had a long conversation with the owners. We had not taken any radiographs yet, but the damage the sign had done was overwhelming. His prognosis was grave, to say the least. But the owners wanted us to take the x-rays and give him the rest of the day.

Off to x-ray we went. Pictures of his entire head, mouth, nose, neck, and chest were done. We were all completely covered in blood, but figured why get cleaned up now. He had a fractured skull, one eye missing, a fractured nose, three fractures in his jaw, 80 percent of his teeth were gone, and a fracture in his shoulder. We did recommend he go to a specialist, but the owners declined. Wow! Where to begin, plus he had not regained consciousness.

We started by cleaning him up, and working on his mouth. We removed the hanging teeth and extracted most of the others. He only had three teeth left when we were finished. Next, we tried to repair the jaw fractures the best we could, all the while continuing to give him a lot of fluids and medications to reduce the swelling in his brain. The doctors felt that was all for the first day since we had no idea if he would even survive. The owners were given an update and still a very poor prognosis, but Duke's heart never faltered.

There were no emergency clinics yet, so we all took turns staying for a few hours with Duke overnight, and by morning, he was still with us, but still unconscious.

After they examined Duke, his vitals had stabilized, but they were so concerned he would never wake up, or if he did, would not be functional. With only one remaining eye, his pupil was not responding to anything yet. The treatment continued with lots of drugs and prayers from his owners.

Then, late on the second day, Duke woke up. He was moaning, but his pupil was responding, and he tried to move, but could not, as the shoulder fracture had not been repaired. We all just stood in amazement. His owners were called, and they came to visit. Duke definitely responded to his owners' voices, and then they were inspired.

Day by day, Duke grew stronger. With his jaw wired, eye removed, and so many facial injuries, we placed a stomach tube and fed him this way. He was then anesthetized, and the shoulder was repaired the best we could. He actually tried to get up the day after his shoulder surgery! This dog was unbelievable. After being in the hospital for ten days, he could stand, with support.

Duke was normally a pretty crazy dog, and now he seemed so mellow. We were surmising this was from the skull fracture as well as the extensive injuries he endured. The wires from his jaw needed to remain for an additional month, so his owners came twice a day to help feed him and provide some much needed support.

It was at week three we had a problem. Duke started to seizure, and it was a major one. Luckily, we were right on it and got him sedated immediately. This was one of the many things the doctors were worried about. Another long and serious conversation between the owners and the doctor ensued. But the owners decided to give him one more week to see what happened.

Duke seizured several more times, but we then added more medication to stop them into his daily routine. And slowly, he seemed to rebound again.

The day arrived when we were to remove the wires from his jaw, and all of us were cautious yet joyful. We were also excited for both Duke and his owners. The procedure went fine, and the jaw had healed; however, there, the three remaining teeth had to be removed.

So, now the real test: could and would he eat? We first offered Duke water, and he just looked at it, but did try and lap it. Then we tried some baby food, and he ate it like he had never missed a meal! We all squealed with delight and still could not imagine how this dog survived.

He was discharged the next day, with many, many instructions, medications, and many follow-ups. As he walked (with a noticeable limp and major head tilt), no teeth, and a face only a mother could love, he looked back, and we all just cried. A miraculous dog with a miraculous staff lead by a miraculous group of doctors.

Duke lived for six more years, but was never allowed to have his head out a window again.

A lesson learned!

For Real

It was February and a very cold and snowy winter. I took a call from Mr. Taylor, a local farmer. He said he had a barn cat that was acting strange and wanted to bring it in. When I questioned him for some details, he said the cat was all beat up and could not walk and was slobbering. My hair raised on my arms. I asked if this cat was vaccinated for rabies, and he said no. I advised him to trap this cat and not touch it. He then replied that he had caught the cat, put it in a box, but did get scratched. I told him to come in immediately.

I alerted Dr. Perkins, and he said he and I would handle this case since we were both vaccinated for rabies.

In came Mr. Taylor with a box taped shut. We took him to an exam room, and we could hear the cat screaming. Mr. Taylor explained that he had many barn cats but had not seen them much lately due to all the snow. Dr. Perkins said he was very concerned this cat had rabies, looked at Mr. Taylor's scratches, and ushered him out the door and ordered him to go see his doctor immediately.

Our first dilemma was how to get the cat out of the box since it was taped. With our heavy gloves and mask on, we slowly removed one piece of tape, and there was a small hole. The cat was still screaming and trying to get out. With his claws, the cat actually made the hole a bit bigger, so we needed to act fast.

Dr. Perkins ran and got an anesthetic drug that you could squirt in the mouth, and when the cat put his mouth to the hole, Dr. Perkins fired the drug. We waited and prayed it would work. After about five minutes, we heard nothing. Very carefully, we took piece by piece of tape off and slowly lifted the lid. We were never so glad to see a cat asleep. It was a white cat, very thin, and had wounds all over it. There was saliva all over its body, and he smelled so bad! It had already been decided to euthanize this cat and have the head examined for rabies.

Dr. Perkins performed the procedure, and we were both so relieved. It was my first (and only) time ever to see a pet with a possible case of active rabies, but Dr. Perkins had seen it quite a few times when he had worked with large animals. We were both very careful not to get anything from the cat on us, and I packaged the cat and drove it to Harrisburg since there was human exposure.

And sure enough, later that day, the health department called and confirmed our suspicions. The cat had rabies! What a mess this was.

Poor Mr. Taylor and his wife had to get post-exposure vaccines, and all the other barn cats had to be trapped and euthanized. He did have a dog, but luckily, he was vaccinated, so a booster was all that was required.

It was several weeks until this work was completed, but our top priority was the Taylors, and they were fine after the vaccines.

A "real" scare, for sure.

Gretchen's Weekend Getaway

Any time you are having construction done in a veterinary hospital, it is not only a major disturbance, but also quite challenging to still work.

We were adding an isolation room and needed to add a door and stairway leading to it. This room was next to our kennel. The kennel was large and housed about fifty dogs.

We had been trying to keep the dogs away from the last section of the runs due to all the noise created, but it came to Friday and we were full with boarders and there were a few dogs in these runs.

One of these dogs was Gretchen, a large and very skittish German Shepherd. Gretchen did come from Germany, and her owners adored her. They had left her to go on a trip back to Germany and were going to be gone for two weeks. They left her on Thursday. Friday morning went fine, and it was not until lunchtime when the animal care attendant came to us and asked us why we took Gretchen. We told her we did not have Gretchen. Her face went white and said she was not in her run. We all rushed to the kennel, and sure enough, she was gone. We searched all over the hospital, and she was nowhere.

The construction crew had left for lunch during this time, but came back, and we questioned them. As we examined the worksite, we found there was a small opening left unblocked, and when the crew left for lunch, we surmised she squeezed through and got out! We were frantic and rushed outside and called and called. We saw nothing. All of the crew and our staff started looking, but I knew how fearful she was and was so worried what she may do.

We looked until suppertime to no avail. We had other staff make flyers, and we went door to door, giving out information. The owners and our entire staff were so distressed as this had never happened before. We felt we needed to continue the search into the night, but we did not find her.

The question arose as to whether or not to call Gretchen's owners. The doctors decided to wait as there was nothing they could do anyway.

Saturday morning came, and the search resumed. All of the construction crew was out with us, but no one had seen her. We expanded the area of the search and still nothing. All day we searched, but no one had seen her. I cannot explain the dismal and empty feeling we all had.

Sunday morning, we caught a break. There was a development about a mile from the practice and someone had spotted her, but when they tried to call her, she just ran again. This was what I feared. She was skittish to begin with, and now running did not help things. We decided to get some smelly lunchmeat, and all meet at the homes. We did see her, and she looked so frightened. We asked the homeowners to open their garage doors, stay inside, and let things quiet down. We all sat at multiple locations, were still, and when she came close to anyone, we threw the lunchmeat, and she gobbled it up! There were two of us sitting in one garage, and she actually came in and ate the lunchmeat and just layed down. She looked so tired. We kept talking to her, and I do believe she recognized us. She actually fell asleep, and we remained still. About thirty minutes later, she woke up and came over to me. As I petted her, she remained calm. We fed her more lunchmeat and then put the leash over her head! Got her!

The elation was overwhelming. As the crew and my staff got together, we rejoiced and then took her back to the hospital. I stayed with her for several hours. She had a few scratches on her, but otherwise unhurt. She continued to eat and do well.

For the remainder of her stay, we kept her in the hospital kennel and leash-walked her outside several times a day. The construction crew finished the wall on Monday, so there could not be any other escapes.

The owners arrived to pick up Gretchen and both the doctors and the construction supervisor met with them and explained what had happened. Needless to say, the construction company paid for everything and took full responsibility. We were all a bit worried how this would all go, but the owners were incredibly grateful for all that we had done and were relieved that Gretchen was fine.

This is the one and only time I have ever experienced losing a pet from any hospital. And I'm okay with that!

We Say the Darnedest Things

Over the years, I have worked with so many amazing people, and I have learned from them all. However, working in a veterinary profession is quite stressful at times, and I've heard things that I never heard anywhere else. Here is a collection of some of my favorites:

A doctor's diagnosis of acute rectalitis and the client responds, "It doesn't look cute to me."

An elderly client calls and reports on her very old dog: "Tikey's dead from the neck down, it won't be long now." An hour later, she calls back and reports, "Now he's dead from the neck up, but I have one question, Do I have to stuff cotton up his rectum before I bury him?"

An owner asked me on a very busy day: "Can't we just fax the deposit?"

On a discharge note for a constipated cat, "Send some Valvoline home."

Dr. Notes, "checked that jaw that possibly swallowed a tooth"

Those nails were twelve inches long, and he said he had another foot on each paw, so he cut them too.

That puppy is having trouble breathing; put it in the microwave.

Yes, I am here to have a Pap smear done on my dog.

New veterinary graduate called a blocked cat as having a penile torsion.

How long did that surgery take from the start to the beginning?

Do I get a discount on a nail trim because my dog only has three legs?

A pharmacist called questioning a phone number that the doctor gave him: 244-70.

Let's try ammonia D for that diarrhea!

Please bring a stew sample in for your cat.

Is your dog here for a limping problem? "No," answered the client, "I just want him checked before he starts!"

When you apply for a lifetime license, you have to go to the whorehouse.

When you go from S/D to C/D, we recommend checking a urinal.

Can you tell if a stool sample is from a male or female dog?

Montana

I have saved the best story for last.

I first met this little guy in January 2002. I was working in my office when three of my technicians brought in this "bundle in a blanket." They gave me "the look" and immediately I knew I was in trouble. They reported this was a seven-week-old Jack Russell terrier who had been hit by a truck three days prior. The owners reported they had put their son in charge of his care and when the boy ran outside, the puppy followed and got hit. They waited and now wanted him euthanized. My staff of veterinarians were upset with the owners' request and asked for ownership.

I unwrapped this little bundle and up look these sorrowful eyes. When I asked the extent of his injuries, I gasped. His back end was pretty well smashed, both rear legs were fractured, his pelvis crushed, and lots of cuts and bruises, and severe internal bruising. He was barely alive, but my terrific staff placed him on life-saving fluids and many medications, and this is what we had to deal with.

Now my technicians knew I had recently put down my sixteen-year-old Jack Russell, and I was quite adamant I would not get another. Thunder, as he was known, was a high-maintenance dog. Seizured all his life, even with medication, barked incessantly, was not very nice to others, and had to be watched very closely.

My first response was, "I don't think I can take this puppy on," and they perfectly understood. But they were also persistent that I just take the puppy home over the weekend, so it would not have to be alone in a kennel. We had a board-certified surgeon that worked Mondays and Thursdays, and they wanted him to evaluate the puppy to see if it was feasible for him to live with any quality. Of course, I did agree to this, and off we went, this little puppy with two splints on his rear legs who could not do anything by himself.

My husband was not surprised as I was always bringing something home to help. This little guy was the most perfect thing all weekend. We had to hold him up to go potty, and he did so like a trooper. We had to hand-feed him and give him many medications and never a whimper. He was in his crate and never made one mess. He did not bark at all; in fact, we wondered if he could.

On Sunday night, we were sitting with the puppy in between us, and my husband said, "We are not really giving him up, are we?" I said I was hooked as well, although we had to face whatever the surgeon said, knowing how severe his injuries were.

Monday came, and Dr. Walker came in and started his exam. Looking at the radiographs, he could not believe this puppy had lived. Back and forth he went, which seemed an eternity to me. Dr. W and I had a great relationship, and I told him I wanted an honest opinion. He turned and picked up the puppy and, of course, got a wet kiss. He told me he could "try" and fix the right leg and pelvis, but the complicating thing was his age. His bones were so soft, and he did not know if any hardware implanted would hold or if the puppy would be able to walk. When I asked if we should try, he said, "This little guy has quite a spirit to live this long, why not?"

That very day, the puppy went into surgery and came out two hours later. Pins were placed in the right rear leg, but he could not do anything with the pelvis. Dr. W said it will have to heal on its own, and we all held our breath. He came out of anesthesia slowly, and remained in the hospital for an additional two days.

I then took him to his "real" home. We had decided not to name the puppy until we knew his fate. We agreed on "Montana," as I am a huge Joe Montana and 49ers fan.

I brought him back and forth every day to the hospital, and he became the hospital favorite. Montana stayed in his little crate in my office and had many treatments, medications, but oh, so much love shown to him daily. We definitely had rough moments as he could not walk at first and really wanted to. We had strict guidelines to follow, and we followed them to a T. Dr. W would check him twice a week and would take more radiographs to monitor.

After four weeks, he felt the right leg was healing, but would never bend again. The second surgery was done, and he did the best he could with hardware. He was also concerned about the hips, and as time went on, three more orthopedic surgeries were completed to help put him back together.

After each surgery, Montana seemed to keep fighting to walk and, eventually, did so. He looks a bit funny, but he knew no different. This dog went through so much and was amazing to watch.

After all the surgeries were complete, Dr. W and I had a heart-to-heart conversation. He informed me that he had now done everything he could, but to realize we would probably only have him for about five years, due to the joint disease he was expecting. He commented that not much research had been done with cases like this and wanted to be honest with me. His advice was to keep exercising him and let him do what he could, but he will eventually lose the control of those rear legs. We placed him on joint supplements right away and followed Dr. W's advice.

Guess what? Montana is now 13 years old! He has been such a joy. He is precious with everyone, including our grandchildren. He rarely barks and is the best dog ever! He has taught us so much, and we are blessed to have him. And, yes, he cannot walk far anymore, but we just carry him, and he is content. He wants no part of a cart, and we have decided that's okay, and yes, we have spoken to Dr. W over the years, and he is so impressed with Montana and glad his prediction was never to be.

Courageous, spirited, and determined are all words to describe this "little bundle of joy" we know as Montana!

About the Author

Julie knew at an early age that helping animals and their owners was her life's passion. Throughout her career, she wore many hats and advanced from a Certified Technician, to Management, and then to Administration. The one common theme in all areas was her ability to connect with her staff, her clients, and their pets, and develop special relationships.

The inspiration for the book came from years of saving amusing stories, bloopers, and interesting characters. Julie would write a story from the year's events and read them at holiday parties and they were always a hit! Many of her staff would say, "You should write a book!" And she finally did!

The goal for this book is to make people smile, laugh, as well as recognize and respect the wonderful work of veterinarians and their staff.

CPSIA information can be obtained
at www.ICGtesting.com
Printed in the USA
BVOW06s2145080218
507690BV00001B/14/P